# GUITAR Worship 1 SONGBOOK Book 1

## Strum & Sing Your Favorite Praise & Worship Songs

**PLAYBACK+**
Speed • Pitch • Balance • Loop

**AUDIO ACCESS INCLUDED**

To access audio visit:
**www.halleonard.com/mylibrary**

4946-5314-7252-9218

Recording Credits:

Vocals: Tonia Emerich and Jim Reith
Guitars: Bryan Mir and Jim Reith
Bass: Eric Hervey
Keyboards: Warren Wiegratz
Drums: Chris Kollman
Recorded, mixed, and mastered by Jim Reith
at Beathouse Music, Milwaukee, WI

ISBN: 978-0-634-07896-5

**HAL•LEONARD®**
CORPORATION

7777 W. BLUEMOUND RD. P.O. BOX 13819 MILWAUKEE, WI 53213

Visit Hal Leonard Online at
**www.halleonard.com**

# Introduction

Welcome to the *Guitar Worship Method Songbook*, a collection of twelve worship favorites arranged for easy guitar chord strumming. If you're a beginning guitarist, you've come to the right place. With the songs in this book, you can practice basic chords and strumming patterns—plus learn how to play twelve Praise and Worship hits!

This book can be used on its own or as a supplement to any guitar method. If you're using it along with the Hal Leonard *Guitar Worship Method* by Garth Heckman, it coordinates with the skills introduced in Book 1. Use the Contents below to see what chords each song contains and to determine when you're ready to play a song. Check out the back of the book for a Chord Chart of all the chords used in this book as well as different strumming patterns you can use.

To play along with the audio, you can remove the easy guitar part by panning your stereo or computer all the way to the left.

# Contents

# Song Structure

The songs in this book have different sections, which may or may not include the following:

## Intro

This is usually a short instrumental section that "introduces" the song at the beginning.

## Verse

This is one of the main sections of a song and conveys most of the storyline. A song usually has several verses, all with the same music but each with different lyrics.

## Chorus

This is often the most memorable section of a song. Unlike the verse, the chorus usually has the same lyrics every time it repeats.

## Bridge

This section is a break from the rest of the song, often having a very different chord progression and feel.

## Solo

This is an instrumental section, often played over the verse or chorus structure.

## Outro

Similar to an intro, this section brings the song to an end.

# Endings & Repeats

Many of the songs have some new symbols that you must understand before playing. Each of these represents a different type of ending.

### 1st and 2nd Endings

These are indicated by brackets and numbers. The first time through a song section, play the first ending and then repeat. The second time through, skip the first ending, and play through the second ending.

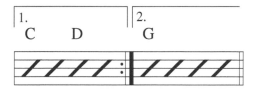

### D.S.

This means "Dal Segno" or "from the sign." When you see this abbreviation above the staff, find the sign (𝄋) earlier in the song and resume playing from that point.

### al Coda

This means "to the Coda," a concluding section in the song. If you see the words "D.S. al Coda," return to the sign (𝄋) earlier in the song and play until you see the words "To Coda," then skip to the Coda at the end of the song, indicated by the symbol: ⊕.

### al Fine

This means "to the end." If you see the words "D.S. al Fine," return to the sign (𝄋) earlier in the song and play until you see the word "Fine."

### D.C.

This means "Da Capo" or "from the head." When you see this abbreviation above the staff, return to the beginning (or "head") of the song and resume playing.

# Breathe

**Words and Music by**
**MARIE BARNETT**

Melody:

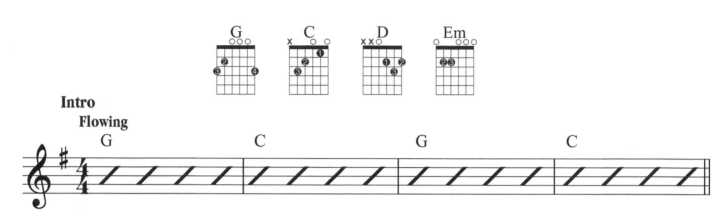

This is — the air — I breathe, —

**Intro**
**Flowing**

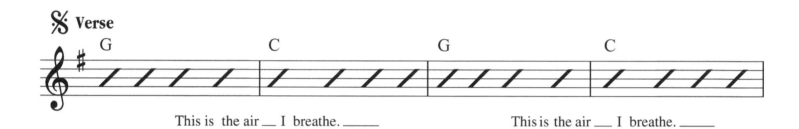

**Verse**

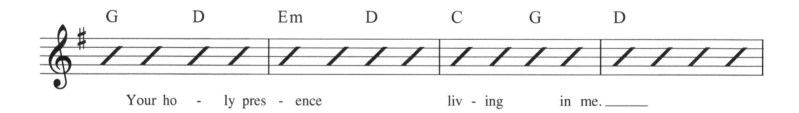

This is the air — I breathe. _____          This is the air — I breathe. _____

Your ho - ly pres - ence          liv - ing          in me. _____

This is my dai - ly bread, _____          This is my dai - ly bread, _____

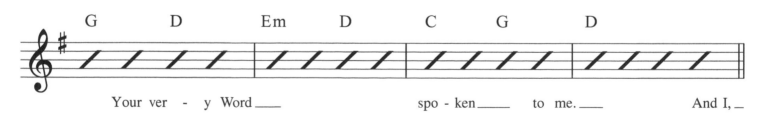

Your ver - y Word _____          spo - ken _____ to me. _____          And I, _

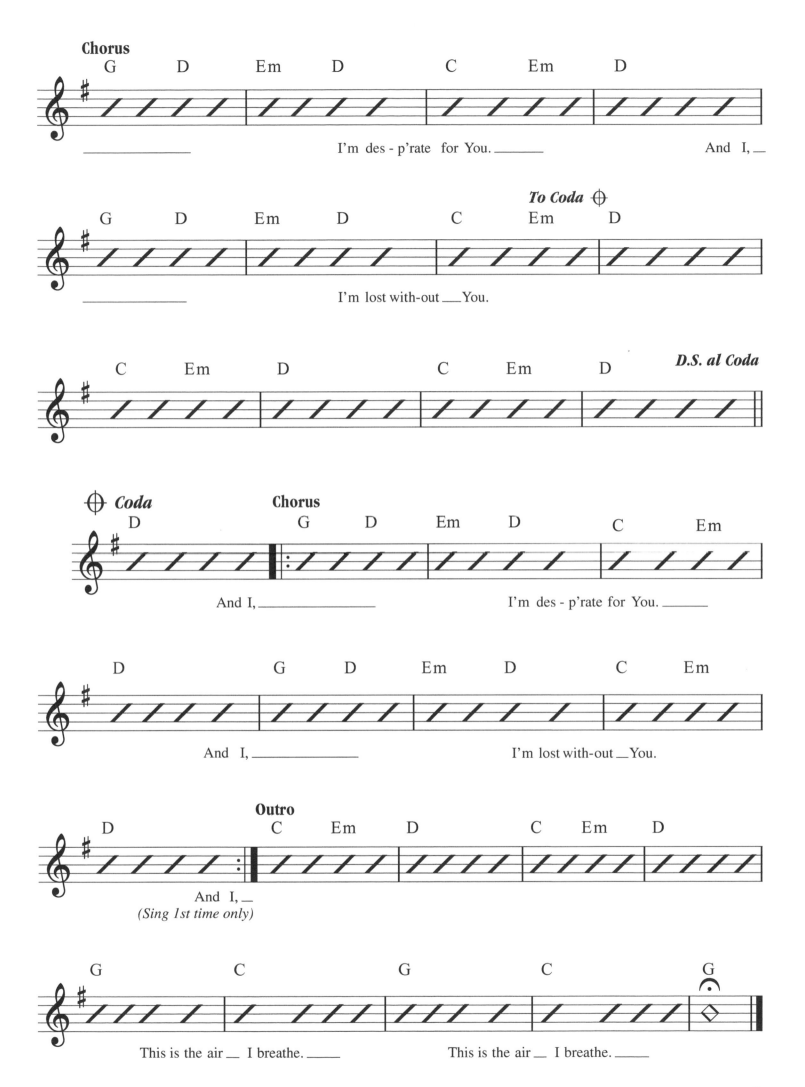

# Better Is One Day

Words and Music by
MATT REDMAN

Melody:

How love-ly is Your dwell-ing place,

**Verse**
**Moderately**

G

1. How love - ly is Your dwell - ing place,
(2.) thing I ask and I would seek:

C      D      G

O Lord Al - might - y,     for my soul longs and
to see Your beau - ty,     to find You in the

D

e - ven faints for You.        For
place Your glo - ry dwells.        One

G              C

here my heart is sat - is - fied     with - in Your pres -
thing I ask and I would seek:     to see Your beau-

D        G

- ence.     I sing be - neath the shad - ow of Your
- ty,     to find You in the place Your glo - ry

# Forever

Words and Music by
CHRIS TOMLIN

Melody:

Give thanks to the Lord, __ our God and King. __

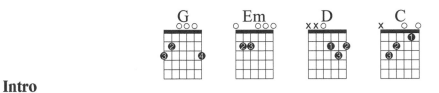

**Intro**
**Joyfully**

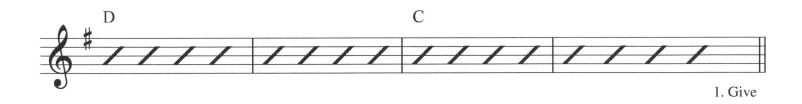

1. Give

**Verse**

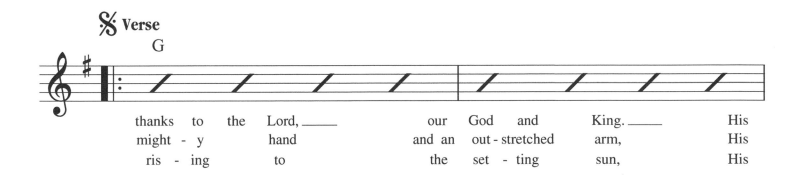

| thanks | to | the | Lord, _____ | | our | God | and | King. _____ | | His |
| might - y | | hand | | and | an | out - stretched | arm, | | | His |
| ris - ing | | to | | the | set - ting | sun, | | | | His |

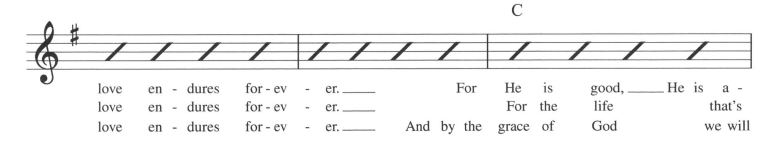

| love | en - dures | for - ev - | er. _____ | | | For | He | is | good, _____ He is a - |
| love | en - dures | for - ev - | er. _____ | | | For the | | life | that's |
| love | en - dures | for - ev - | er. _____ | And | by the | grace of | | God | we will |

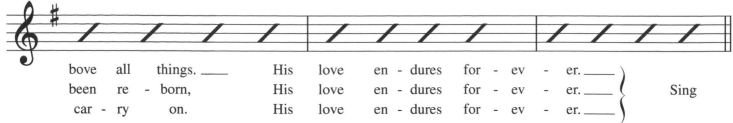

bove all things. ____ His love en - dures for - ev - er. ____
been re - born, His love en - dures for - ev - er. ____
car - ry on. His love en - dures for - ev - er. ____ Sing

**Pre-Chorus**

D                                                                 1.  C

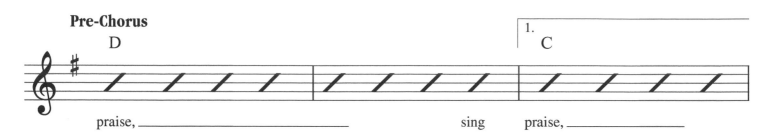

praise, _____ sing praise, _____

2.  C

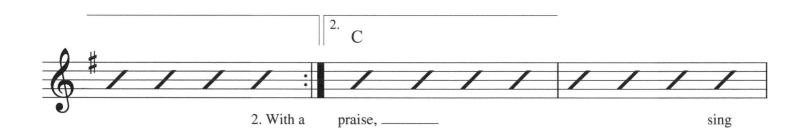

2. With a    praise, _____                                          sing

D                                              C

praise, _____ sing praise. _____

**Chorus**

G

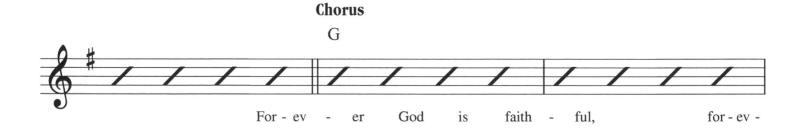

For - ev - er God is faith - ful, for - ev -

Em                                              D

- er God is strong, ____ for - ev - er God is with ____

10

*To Coda* ⊕
C

_____ us,       for - ev  -  er, _____                    for - ev -

*D.S. al Coda*
*(take 2nd ending)*
G

- er. _____                                        3. From the

⊕ *Coda*
C                                         **Outro**
                                          G

- er.                              For - ev  -  er   God    is    faith-

Em

- ful,        for - ev  -  er   God    is    strong, _____        for - ev -

D                                              C

- er   God    is    with _____ us,              for - ev  -  er,

G

for - ev  -  er.

# Open the Eyes of My Heart

**Words and Music by PAUL BALOCHE**

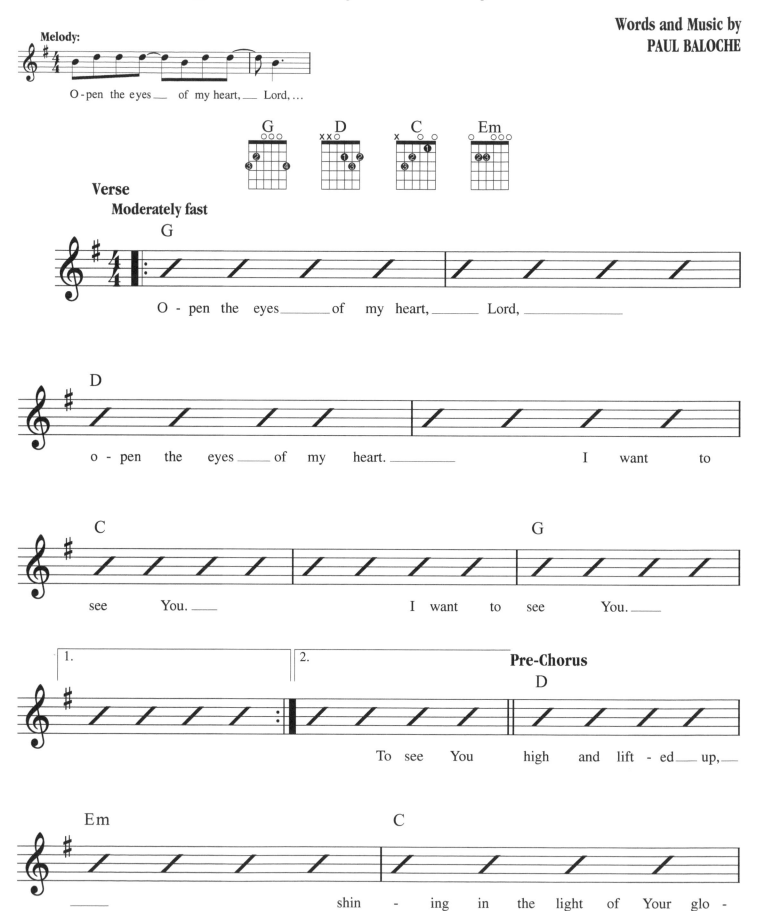

Melody:

O-pen the eyes of my heart, Lord, ...

**Verse**
**Moderately fast**

G

O - pen the eyes of my heart, Lord,

D

o - pen the eyes of my heart. I want to

C                    G

see You. I want to see You.

1.

2.    **Pre-Chorus**

D

To see You high and lift - ed up,

Em                    C

shin - ing in the light of Your glo -

-ry. _____        Pour out    Your    pow'r    and    love _____

*To Coda* ⊕             *D.C. al Coda*
*(take repeats)*

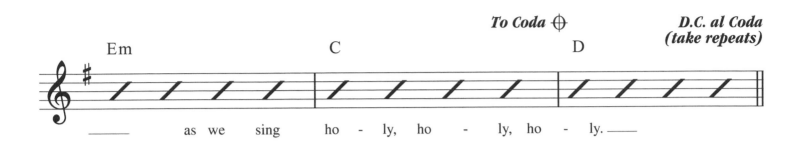

_____    as   we   sing   ho  -  ly,   ho  -  ly,   ho  -  ly. _____

⊕ *Coda*

**Chorus**

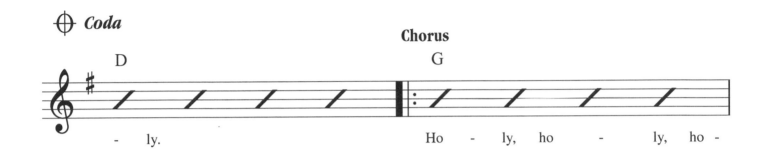

-ly.             Ho  -  ly,   ho  -  ly,   ho  -

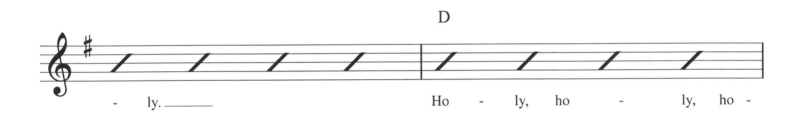

-ly. _____       Ho  -  ly,   ho  -  ly,   ho  -

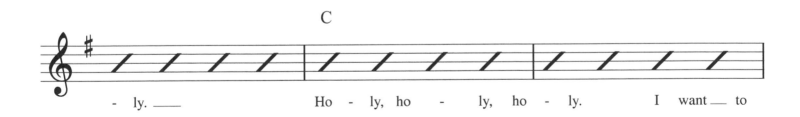

-ly. _____       Ho  -  ly,   ho  -  ly,   ho  -  ly.     I   want _ to

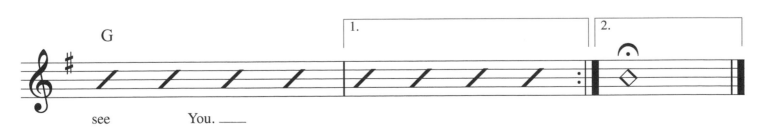

see      You. _____

# Here I Am to Worship

Words and Music by
TIM HUGHES

Light of the World, You stepped down in-to dark-ness,...

**Verse**

**Moderately slow**

1. Light of the World, You stepped down in-to dark-ness,
2. King of all days, oh so high-ly ex-alt-ed,

o-pened my eyes, let me ____ see.
glo-ri-ous in heav-en a-bove.

Beau-ty that made this ____ heart a-dore ____ You,
Hum-bly You came to the earth You cre-at-ed,

hope of a life spent with ____ You.
all for love's sake be-came ____ poor.

Here I am to

**Chorus**

wor-ship, here I am to bow down, here I am to

# You Are My King
## (Amazing Love)

**Words and Music by**
**BILLY JAMES FOOTE**

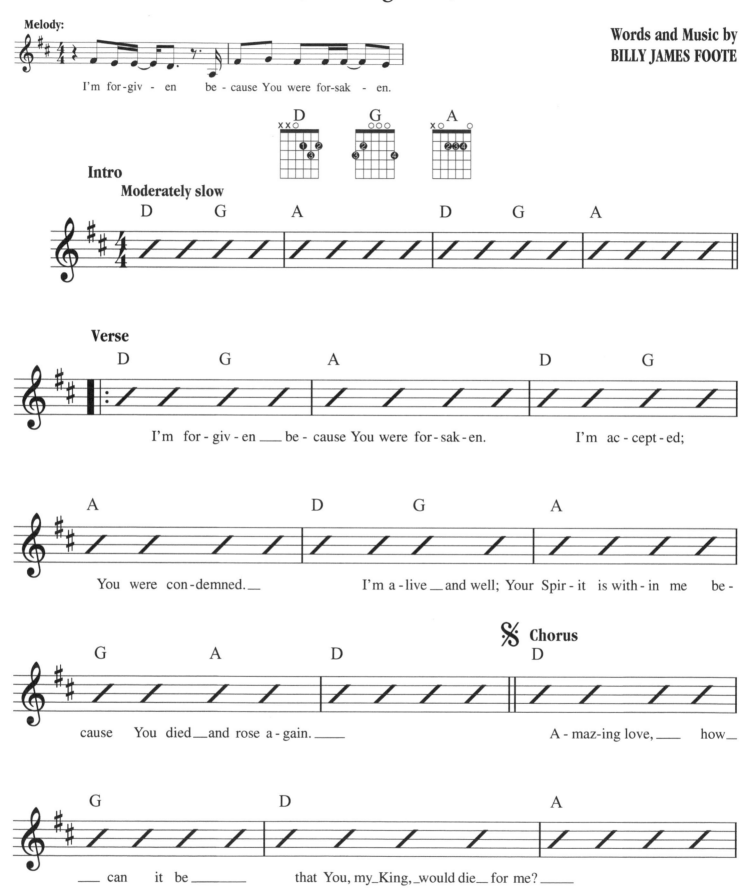

**Melody:**

I'm for-giv-en be-cause You were for-sak-en.

**Intro**

**Moderately slow**

**Verse**

I'm for-giv-en ___ be-cause You were for-sak-en. I'm ac-cept-ed;

You were con-demned. ___ I'm a-live ___ and well; Your Spir-it is with-in me be-

**Chorus**

cause You died ___ and rose a-gain. ___ A-maz-ing love, ___ how ___

___ can it be ___ that You, my ___ King, ___ would die ___ for me? ___

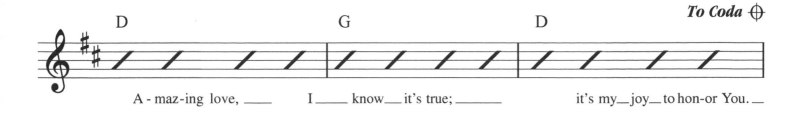

D         G         D

A - maz-ing love, ___ I ___ know ___ it's true; ___ it's my ___ joy ___ to hon-or You. ___

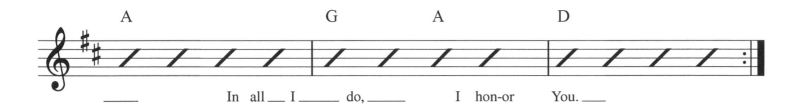

A         G    A      D

___ In all ___ I ___ do, ___ I hon-or You. ___

**Bridge**

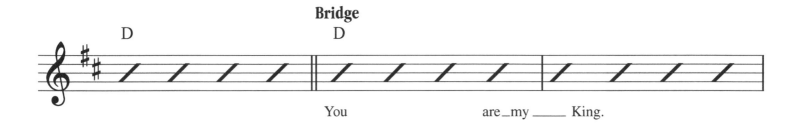

D         D

You      are ___ my ___ King.

You      are ___ my ___ King.    Je - sus, You      are ___ my ___

***D.S. al Coda***

___ King.    Je - sus, You      are ___ my ___ King.

⊕ **Coda**

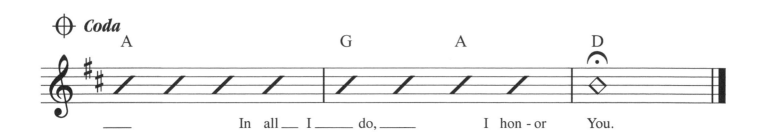

A         G      A      D

___ In all ___ I ___ do, ___ I hon - or You.

# Blessed Be Your Name

Words and Music by
MATT REDMAN and BETH REDMAN

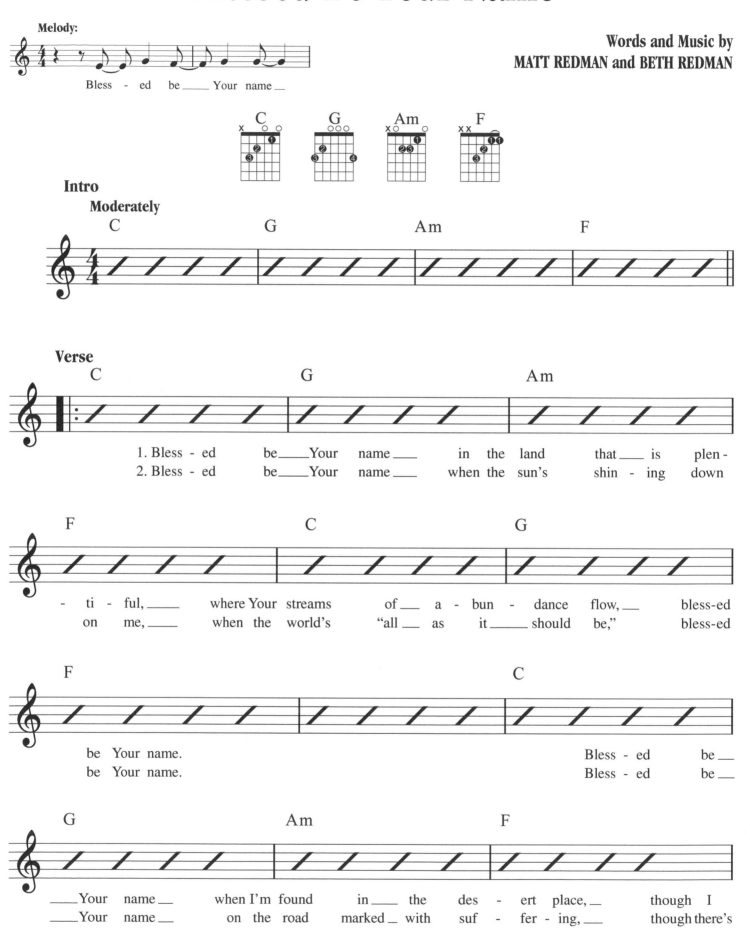

C            G            F

walk    through \_\_ the   wil - der - ness,\_\_    bless - ed \_\_ be Your name.
pain     in \_\_   the    of - fer - ing, \_\_    bless - ed \_\_ be Your name.

**𝄋 Pre-Chorus**

C            G            Am

Ev-'ry bless - ing   You   pour   out   I'll    turn   back   to

F            C            G

praise.       When   the   dark - ness   clos - es   in,   Lord,

**Chorus**

Am          F          C

still   I   will    say:    Bless - ed be the    name    of \_\_ the \_\_ Lord, \_\_

G          Am          F

\_\_    bless - ed be Your   name.      Bless - ed be the

*To Coda* ⊕

C          G          Am    G

name    of \_\_ the \_\_ Lord, \_\_    bless - ed be Your glor - ri - ous name. \_\_

1.         2.       **Bridge**

F         F         C         G

\_\_                 You   give   and   take   a - way,    You

Am      F      C

give   and   take   a - way.     My   heart   will   choose   to

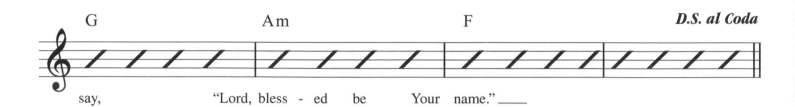

G      Am      F      **D.S. al Coda**

say,    "Lord, bless - ed   be   Your   name." ____

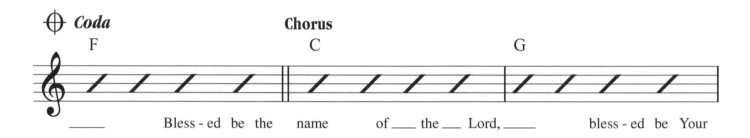

⊕ *Coda*      **Chorus**

F      C      G

____    Bless - ed   be   the   name    of ___ the ___ Lord, ____    bless - ed   be   Your

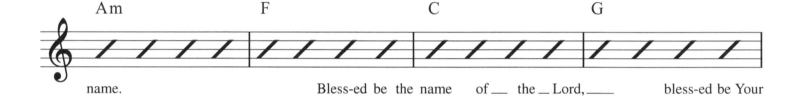

Am      F      C      G

name.      Bless-ed   be   the   name    of __ the __ Lord, ____    bless-ed   be   Your

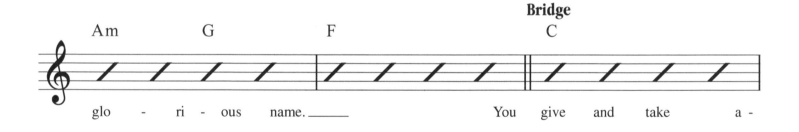

Am   G      F      **Bridge**

     C

glo   -   ri   -   ous   name. _____    You   give   and   take   a -

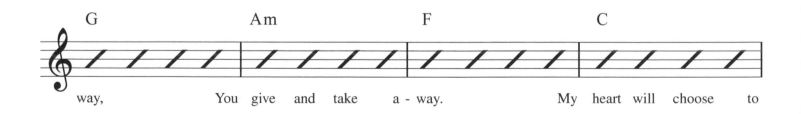

G      Am      F      C

way,    You   give   and   take   a - way.     My   heart   will   choose   to

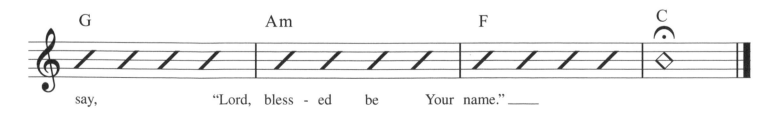

G      Am      F      C

say,    "Lord, bless - ed   be   Your   name." ____

# My Redeemer Lives

Words and Music by
REUBEN MORGAN

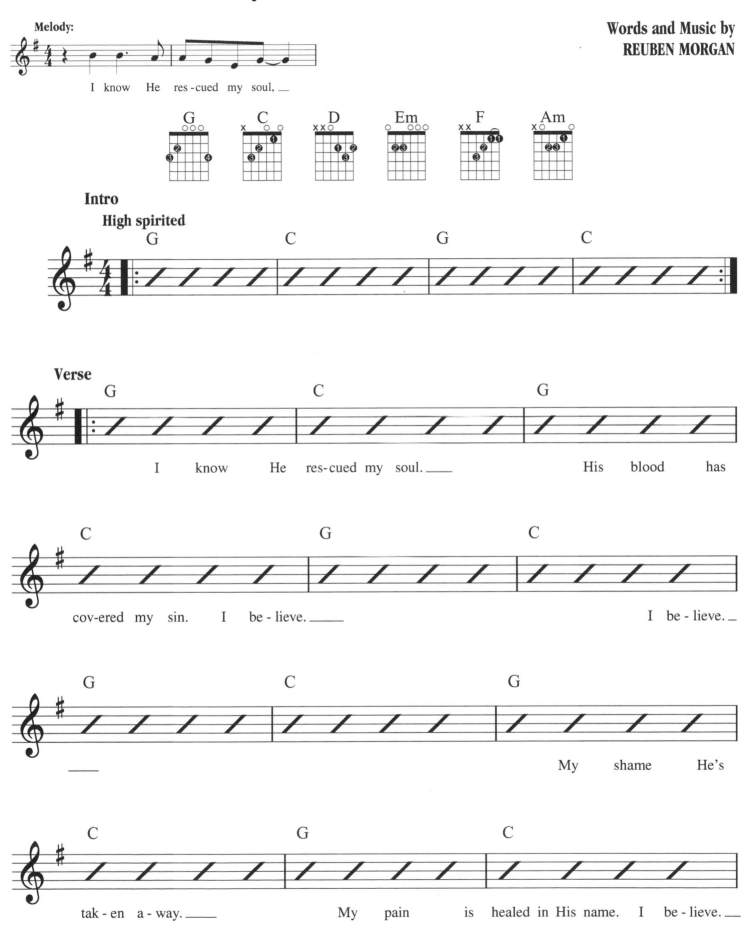

**Melody:**

I know He res-cued my soul, —

**Intro**
**High spirited**

G          C          G          C

**Verse**

G          C          G

I know He res-cued my soul. — His blood has

C          G          C

cov-ered my sin. I be-lieve. — I be-lieve. —

G          C          G

— My shame He's

C          G          C

tak-en a-way. — My pain is healed in His name. I be-lieve. —

G | C | G

I be - lieve. _____

**Pre-Chorus**

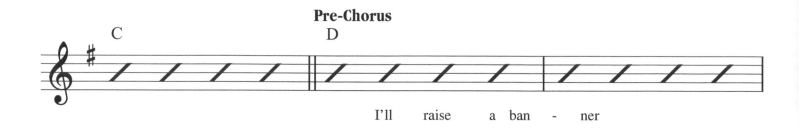

C | D

I'll raise a ban - ner

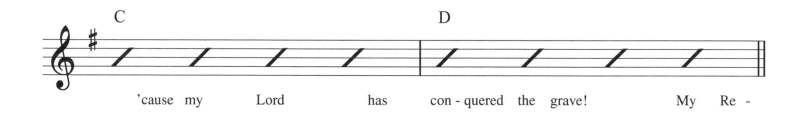

C | D

'cause my Lord has con - quered the grave! My Re -

## 𝄋 Chorus

G | C | Em

deem - er lives! _____ My Re - deem - er lives! _

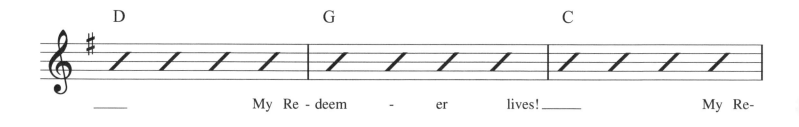

D | G | C

_____ My Re - deem - er lives! _____ My Re-

*To Coda* ⊕

1.

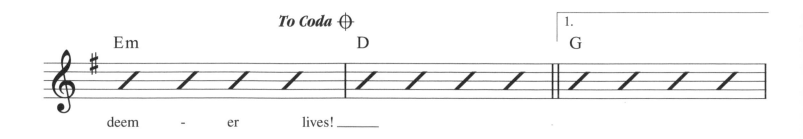

Em | D | G

deem - er lives! _____

# Come, Now Is the Time to Worship

Words and Music by
BRIAN DOERKSEN

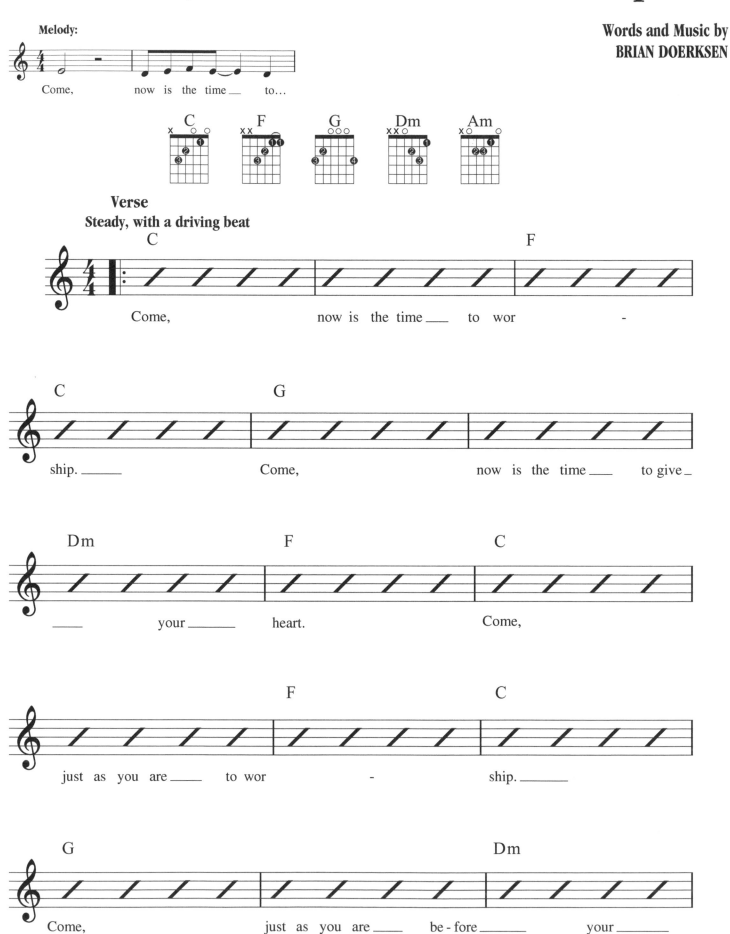

**Verse**
**Steady, with a driving beat**

Come, now is the time __ to wor - ship. __ Come, now is the time __ to give __ your __ heart. Come, just as you are __ to wor - ship. __ Come, just as you are be - fore __ your __

F       *To Coda* ⊕   C

God.         Come.

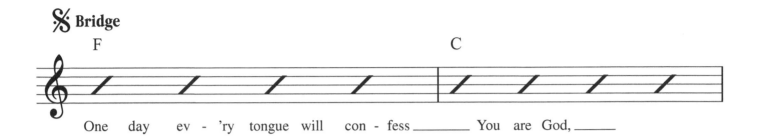

𝄋 **Bridge**

F                     C

One day ev - 'ry tongue will con - fess _____ You are God, _____

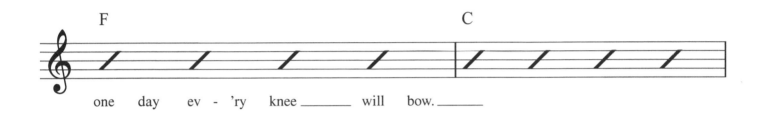

F                     C

one day ev - 'ry knee _____ will bow. _____

F             Am             Dm

Still the great-est trea-sure re-mains ___ for those ___ who glad - ly choose ___ You now. ___

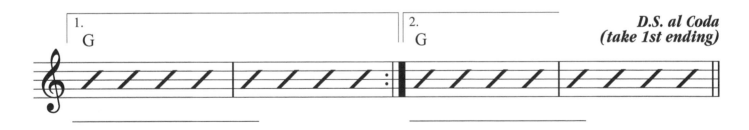

1.
G

2.
G

***D.S. al Coda
(take 1st ending)***

⊕ *Coda*
**Outro**

C                       F   *Play 7 times*   C

Come.                        Come.

# Lord, Reign in Me

Words and Music by
BRENTON BROWN

Melody:

O - ver all the earth ___ You ___ reign on ___ high,...

C  G  F  Am  Dm

**Verse**
**Steadily**

C                    G                    F                    G

1. O - ver all the ___ earth ___ You reign on ___ high, ___
2. O - ver ev - 'ry thought, o - ver ev - 'ry word,

C                    G                    F                    G

___ ev - 'ry moun - tain ___ stream, ___ ev - 'ry sun - set ___ sky.
may my life re - flect the beau - ty of my Lord.

Am                   G                    F                    G

But my one re - quest, ___ Lord, my on - ly ___ aim ___
You mean more to me than an - y earth - ly thing, ___

Dm                                        F                    G

___ is that You'd reign in me a - gain. ___
___ so won't You reign in me a - gain? ___

**℅ Chorus**

C                    G                    F                    G

___ { Lord, reign in ___ me, ___ reign in Your ___ pow'r,

o - ver all my _____ dreams, _____ in my dark - est hour. ___

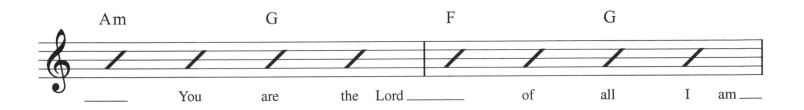

_____ You are the Lord _____ of all I am ___

**To Coda** ⊕ | 1.

_____ so won't You reign in me a - gain? ___

___

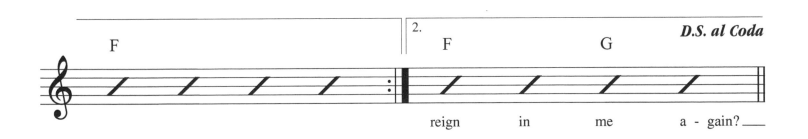

2.

**D.S. al Coda**

reign in me a - gain? ___

⊕ **Coda**

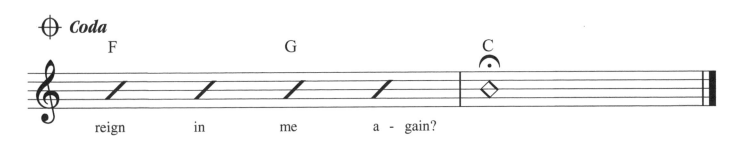

reign in me a - gain?

# Days of Elijah

Words and Music by
ROBIN MARK

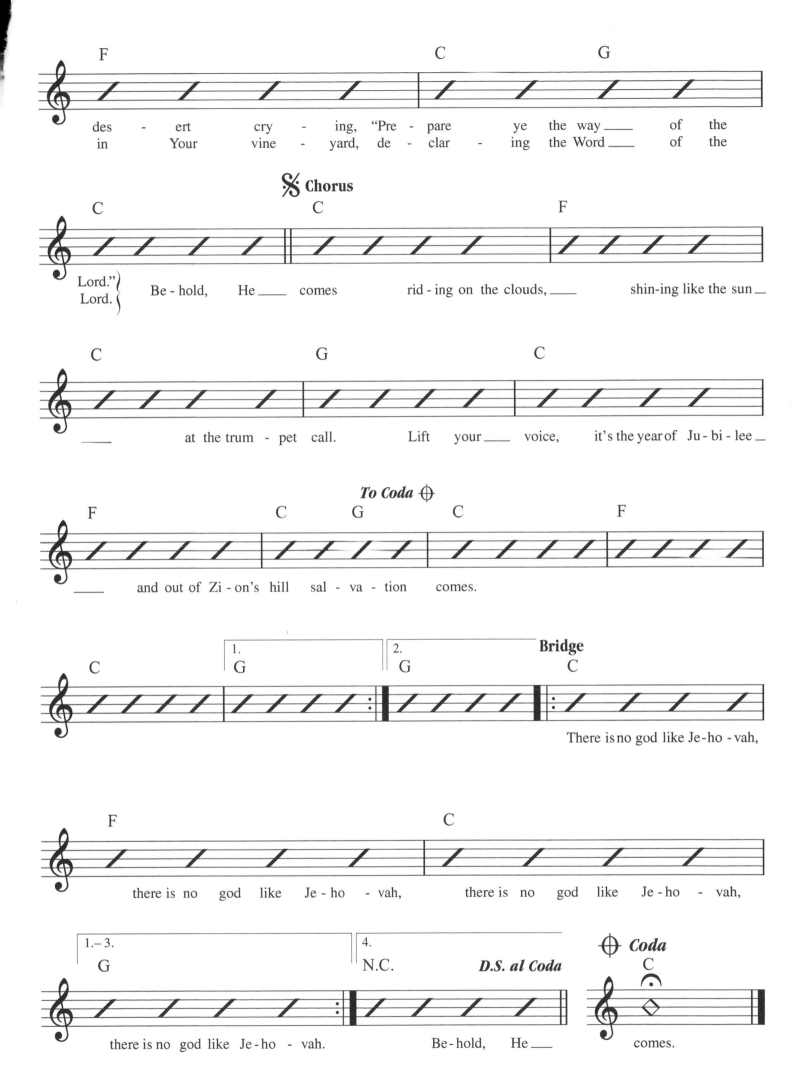

# I Could Sing of Your Love Forever

Words and Music by
MARTIN SMITH

Melody:

O - ver ___ the moun - tains and ___ the sea...

**C   Dm   F   G   Am   Em**

**Verse**
**Moderately**

**C**

O - ver ___ the moun - tains and ___ the sea    Your riv - er runs ___ with love ___ for me,

**Dm**                          **F**            **G**

and I ___ will o - pen up ___ my heart ___    and let the Heal - er set ___ me free.

**C**

I'm hap - py to ___ be in ___ the truth,    and I ___ will dai - ly lift ___ my hands,

**Dm**                          **F**            **G**

for I ___ will al - ways sing ___ of when Your love came down. ___

**𝄋 Chorus**
**C**                                         **G**

I could sing of Your love ___ for - ev - er.

# Strum Patterns

The first responsibility of a chord player is to *play the right chord on time*. Keep this in mind as you learn new strumming patterns. No matter how concerned you might be with right-hand strumming, getting to the correct chord with your left hand is more important. If necessary, leave the old chord early in order to arrive at the new chord on time.

That said, here are some suggested strum patterns. Choose one that challenges you, and practice it. Whenever you learn a new chord or progression, try putting it into one of these patterns. Also, try applying these to the songs in this book.

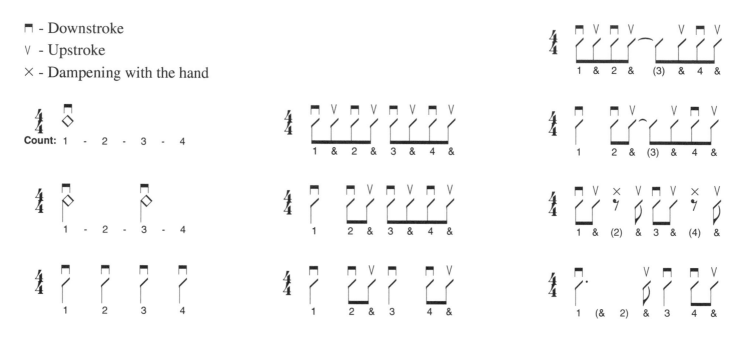

∏ - Downstroke
V - Upstroke
× - Dampening with the hand

Eighth notes in the above strums may be played even or uneven ("swung") depending on the style of music.

# Chord Chart

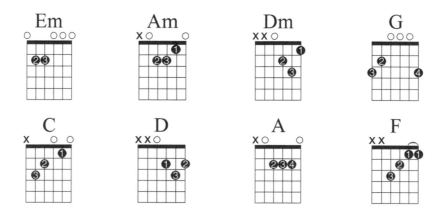